AF221165

1

Astragalus Root

Anti-Aging Secret Revealed After 2000 Years

Peter Carl Simons

Bibliografische Information der Deutschen Nationalbibliothek:

Die Deutsche Nationalbibliothek verzeichnet diese Publikation in der Deutschen Nationalbibliografie; detaillierte bibliografische Daten sind im Internet über http://dnb.dnb.de abrufbar.

Herstellung und Verlag: BoD –
Books on Demand, Norderstedt

ISBN: 978-3-7526-4138-7

Introduction

By using this book, you accept this disclaimer in full.

No advice

The book contains information. The information is not advice and should not be treated as such.

No representations or warranties

To the maximum extent permitted by applicable law and subject to section below, we exclude all representations, warranties, undertakings and guarantees relating to the book.

Without prejudice to the generality of the foregoing paragraph, we do not represent, warrant, undertake or guarantee:

- that the information in the book is correct, accurate, complete or non-misleading.

- that the use of the guidance in the book will lead to any particular outcome or result.

Limitations and exclusions of liability

The limitations and exclusions of liability set out in this section and elsewhere in this disclaimer: are subject to section 6 below; and govern all liabilities arising under the disclaimer or in relation to the book, including liabilities arising in contract, in tort (including negligence) and for breach of statutory duty.

We will not be liable to you in respect of any losses arising out of any event or events beyond our reasonable control.

We will not be liable to you in respect of any business losses, including without limitation loss of or damage to profits, income, revenue, use, production, anticipated savings, business, contracts, commercial opportunities or goodwill.

We will not be liable to you in respect of any loss or corruption of any data, database or software.

We will not be liable to you in respect of any special, indirect or consequential loss or damage.

Exceptions

Nothing in this disclaimer shall: limit or exclude our liability for death or personal injury resulting from negligence; limit or exclude our liability for fraud or fraudulent misrepresentation; limit any of our liabilities in any way that is not permitted under applicable law; or exclude any of our liabilities that may not be excluded under applicable law.

Severability

If a section of this disclaimer is determined by any court or other competent authority to be unlawful and/or unenforceable, the other sections of this disclaimer continue in effect.

If any unlawful and/or unenforceable section would be lawful or enforceable if part of it were deleted, that part will be deemed to be deleted, and the rest of the section will continue in effect.

Law and jurisdiction

This disclaimer will be governed by and construed in accordance with Swiss law, and any disputes relating to this disclaimer will be subject to the exclusive jurisdiction of the courts of Switzerland.

Contents

Aging of a human being

Every 11 months, the body renews all of its cells. Why, then, we still develop signs of aging? Scientists say you can not completely excrete all aged cells. So, each of us is interested in prolonging the life. Drawing up individual programs for physical improvement and nutrition of men and women between 24 and 40 years old can independently deal with premature aging.

What are Old age and aging? Old age –is inevitable, coming to replace the maturity period of the life of humans and animals, characterized by a decrease in compensatory capabilities and reactivity. Old age is the result of a dynamic process called aging.

Aging –a long biological process of age-related changes in the body that starts long before retirement and is inevitably leading to a gradually increasing restriction of the adaptive capacity of the organism and increase the likelihood of death. Age-related changes that occur at the cellular, sub-cellular and molecular levels, in different organs and systems are developing at different speeds and uneven.

Aging is internally inconsistent. Along with the reduction, the weakening of one process is strengthening others. Thanks to these new developing compensatory mechanisms that could, however, only marginally to replace the previously existing compensation mechanisms.

There are two types of aging –physiological, referred to above, and pathological (premature). Premature or pathological aging occurs at a relatively young age as a result of long-term effects on the human body of some harmful factors external and internal environment (illness, injury, severe domestic and industrial conditions, alcoholism, unfavorable heredity and so forth.), Accelerates the normal, physiological aging.

The nature and course of physiological aging are largely determined by the length of the natural life of human life. It is considered that the potential human lifespan should be more than 100 years. However, it is still rare. Average life expectancy for men and women changes according to their nativity, origin, and other health conditions. The study of age-related changes in various organs and tissues of the human body led to the conclusion that older people are aged between 60 and 74 years old and the period begins after 75 years. People 90 years and older are called longevity.

What prevents a man to live a life of possible longevity? There are many theories to explain the cause of aging. Followers of some theories to explain the onset of old age changes in any internal organs or systems: the endocrine system, the nervous system, connective tissue. Adherents of other theories recognize the leading factor in the aging self-poisoning organism exchange products. Many researchers have suggested the accumulation over the life cycle of the body's synthesis of so-called errors of proteins and nucleic acids, which is reflected in the structure of the molecules of these compounds.

Human Aging is characterized by significant changes in various organs and systems; changes of the appearance, mentality, behavior. Loss of smoothness of the movements, limited joint mobility, decreased muscle strength, hair turns gray, they are rare and fragile, the skin thins and becomes less elastic and wrinkles appear, reduced mental capacity, there is easier fatigue, memory loss occurs, disturbed sleep, the sensitivity of organs and tissues to nervous influences is reduced and so on.

In old age, there are significant changes in the function of the cardiovascular system.

Heart rate slows down, vascular reactions become more inert. Arteries become dense, brittle and crimped. Blood cells and red bone marrow is the spongy bone does not undergo any significant morphological changes. The lymph nodes develop atrophic processes. In the lungs of old people shows senile changes, thereby reducing their breathing capacity.

As we age, our body disrupted the activities of the gastrointestinal tract. The mucous membrane of the mouth becomes thinner, teeth fall out. The stomach is reduced in the elderly; it is thinned mucosa, wrinkles and smoothens. Teeth loss worsens machining food in the oral cavity. Admission to the gastrointestinal tract poorly chewed food creates unfavorable conditions for its digestion. Upcoming changes to the old age of the digestive system function can be one of the causes of vitamin A deficiency.

Pathological processes flow slowly and slug-gishly. This is the reason for the hidden course of the disease; they are often asymp-tomatic, indicating an overall decline in lev-els of reactive processes. Accepted provide the disease, the development of which is di-rectly related to the aging process.

Doctors say that the aging of a man is a multi-faceted, complex and genetically con-ditioned process. You cannot prevent it, but you can slow down. The person becomes old and the very old only if it allows to itself: can be old and of 30-40 years and 90-100 years – only the elderly. Each of us has three age groups: astrological (calendar), biological and psychological.

The calendar age determined by the number of years lived, biological –based on the func-tional state of internal organs, the circula-tory system, etc. and your psychological age of a person determines independently, fo-cusing on the subjective feelings. In his youth, usually psychological age is over-stated, but over the years –on the contrary.

Anyhow, most of the people are really interested in finding a way to stop or reverse the aging process. That is why many people try out new methods of therapies, exercises, and diets. While general population is busy with their own discoveries and inventions, the scientists found out something really interesting about aging. After several years of this discovery, came the next great discovery of stopping and reversing human aging. After all, it was a discovery of something we already knew, but, has been kept as a secret for 2000 years!

Telomeres & Telomerase; What are they?

Telomeres – is the end portions of the chromosomes that perform a protective function. There is the so-called Hayflick limit, which is the maximum number of times a normal human cell population can divide until cell division stops. This is coupled with a reduction of telomere length –the number of divisions of somatic cells approximately equal to 50, after which the cells begin to show signs of aging. Studies have shown that DNA is able to recover the enzyme telomerase, which affects telomeres, by restoring their original length.

The new technology in the modern world has been able to produce a modified RNA, which carries a gene that can deactivate the telomerase enzyme and is called as the telomerase reverse transcriptase gene (TERT).

Introduction of ribonucleic acid greatly increases telomerase activity for 1-2 days, for which she actively lengthens telomeres, and programmed splits RNA. The resultant cells behave like "young" and share many times more intense than the control group cells.

Thus, it was possible to lengthen telomeres over 1000 nucleotides, which is equivalent to several years of human life. What is important, the process is completely safe for health and does not lead to uncontrolled cell division: the immune system simply does not have time to respond to the introduction into the body of RNA, which completely breaks down. The discovery will help to increase the number of cells for research of medicines and modeling of diseases, and in the future, and to prolong life.

Many modern literatures define telomeres as specialized terminal regions of linear chromosomal DNA consisting of repetitive short nucleotide sequences. This definition is incomplete. The structure of telomeres includes many proteins that specifically bind to telomeric DNA repeats. Thus, telomeres (as well as all other regions of eukaryotic chromosomes) that are constructed from Deoxyribonucleic acid are a piece of DNA.

The existence of special structures at the ends of chromosomes was postulated in 1938 by Nobel laureate Barbara McClintock and Hermann Muller. Independently of each other, they found that fragmentation of chromosomes (under the influence of X-rays) and the appearance of their other ends that lead to chromosomal rearrangements and chromosome degradation. But, a region of chromosome adjacent to their natural ends remained safe. When these ends are deprived, the chromosomes began to multiply in a high frequency, which leads to severe genetic abnormalities. Therefore, they concluded, the natural ends of linear chromosomes are protected by special structures. G. Muller suggested calling these ends as "telomeres" (from the Greek telos-End and meros-part).

In subsequent years, it was found out that the telomeres not only prevent degradation and fusion of chromosomes (and thus maintain the integrity of the host cell genome) but also seems to be responsible for the attachment of chromosomes to the special intranuclear structures (a sort of skeleton of the cell nucleus), called the nuclear matrix. Thus, telomeres play an important role in the creation of a specific architecture and the internal order of the cell nucleus. Moreover, we show that the presence of special telomeric DNA at the ends of chromosomes can solve the replication problem of DNA.

But there was a question whether there are ways to return short telomeres to its original length? In 1971, scientist Alexey Matveevich

Olovnikov suggested that the human body has not only the telomeres but, also the enzyme that they can build them up – it is called as telomerase.

Telomerase is an enzyme that is synthesized by tandemly repeated DNA segments. Thus, it relates to a class of DNA polymerases, and it was found that telomerase is an RNA-dependent DNA polymerase or reverse transcriptase. The enzyme of this class, which synthesizes DNA on an RNA template, is very well known to molecular biologists. They are contained in coded and retroviruses (such as human immunodeficiency virus that causes AIDS) and serve for the synthesis of DNA copies of their genome, which is represented by RNA retrovirus.

This enzyme is in the body of each of us, but it is "dormant" in most of the cells or has a low activity, which is further attenuated with age. But there are exceptions; in the human germ cells (sperm and eggs) high telomerase activity is observed throughout the life and similarly, in the stem cells that can divide indefinitely. Moreover, stem cells always have the opportunity to give two daughter cells, one of which will stem ("immortal"), and the other will enter into a process of differentiation (gain their functional purpose in the body). That is why they are a constant source of various cells in the body.

Once a germ cell or a descendant of a stem cell begins to differentiate, telomerase activity starts declining, and then telomeres begin to shorten. In cells where differentiation is complete, telomerase activity drops to zero, and with each cell division, they inevitably near the time when all will cease to divide. Following this come the crisis and most cells die.

Telomerase activity is considered as a possible marker of physiological reserves and the length of telomeres –a "cellular clock", limiting the number of possible cell divisions, and hence it is the duration of a healthy life. Nobel laureate Elizabeth Blackburn in 2009 suggested that telomerase, in addition to lengthening the ends of telomeres protects the structure, the violation of which also threatens to cell death. Another interesting fact is that the individual structural elements of telomerase also signify their functional purpose in the cell.

For example, bone marrow stem cells give rise to hematopoiesis (the process of different kinds of blood cells). Once sexual or descendants of stem cells begin to differentiate, telomerase activity is declining, and their telomeres begin to shorten. In cells where differentiation is complete, telomerase activity drops to zero, and, as we have already noted, with each cell division, they inevitably nearing of senescent (stop dividing). After this phase, most of the cells are killed. This pattern is typical for the vast majority of the known cultures of eukaryotic cells. However, there are rare but important exceptions: telomerase activity is detected in such a "mortal" cells such as macrophages and leukocytes.

It has recently been found that normal somatic cells because of the lack of the telomerase activity have completely suppressed expression of its catalytic subunit gene (reverse transcriptase). Other components of telomerase, including the telomerase RNA, are formed in these cells, although in smaller quantities than in their "immortal" progenitors, but always (or as they say, constitutively).

In normal somatic cells telomerase, reverse transcriptase genes were made using special vectors constructed from the viral DNA. The level of gene expression in eukaryotic cells depends on many factors, including the proteins –the transcription factors that bind to specialized DNA regions located on chromosome adjacent to the gene. The genomes of viruses, which need to quickly reproduce in a host cell, carry DNA segments that can be many times enhance expression of a gene. The researchers made sure that their designs gene telomerase reverse transcriptase person was surrounded by just such sections of viral DNA.

Telomeres – Cell Aging & Cancer

Telomeres play an important role in the process of cell division;

- They ensure the stability of the genome:
- Protect the chromosomes from fusion and degradation during replication;
- Ensure the structural integrity of the endings of chromosomes;
- Protect cells from mutations, aging, and death.

Scientists have discovered that a cell ceases to divide when at least length of one telomere reaches the maximum possible short length. Nature has created a clever mechanism to protect our genome and prevent possible mutations, the cell stops dividing when the protection ends.

We begin to age from the moment of our conception. The cells begin to divide as soon as they begin to form tissues and organs. We are born, grown up, and then comes the period of aging, where our organs and tissues wear out, skin wrinkles and the physical strength reduces. All these features are explained as a result of some aging mechanisms and thereby the theories of aging were introduced to the world. Here are the three main theories of aging according to science:

Theory	Features	Purpose of correction

Free radical	The number of free radicals increases in the aging process, leading to oxidative stress, damaging vital macromolecules inside the cells.	The fight against oxidative stress

Endocrine	Morphological and functional changes in organs occur due to deficiency of hormones, among which the most significant is the deficiency of sex hormones	Eliminating hormone deficiency

Telomeric	Each time a cell divides the telomeres are reduced, reaching at some point a critical level at which the cell cannot divide anymore – it is called as aging or dying	Recover critically short telomere length, preventing their erosion

In the middle of the last century, the focus of all scientists has gone to the theory of telomeres. After the discovery of "Hayflick limit", it was recognized that the cells that no longer divide, become senescent (aged), waiting for three scenarios:

- First –to fall into anabiotic state where the cell does not live or die, but, remain releasing waste products;
- Second option –is to die (by apoptosis);
- And the third option –to mutate and develop into cancer. That is why, when a cell gets old, the risk of developing cancer increases.

What are the diseases develop in people with shorter telomeres in the first place? Let us have a look;

The most common are the diseases of the cardiovascular system. Those who are with short telomeres have 3 times higher risk of sudden death from heart attack and development of coronary artery disease. Furthermore, several researches revealed the relationship of short telomeres with the development of hypertension and chronic heart failure.

There is plenty of evidence that telomere shortening is associated with cancer development. Patients with diskeratosis (a congenital abnormality), has a 1000-times increased risk of developing cancer of the tongue, and about 200 times –the risk of developing acute myeloid leukemia. In addition, congenital diskeratosis causes premature aging of the skin. Furthermore, there is evidence of the relationship between telomere length and the risk of dementia and diabetes.

It is now known that reactivation of telomerase extends replicative life of somatic cells, as example it increases the number of divisions. However, this is exactly what happens in the tumors and leads them to a malignant growth.

It has always been a question how a person can achieve human longevity and slow aging, at the same time without causing the development of malignant tumors?

One choice is the reactivation of telomerase in proliferative cells with simultaneous stimulation of normal oncosupressors (the genes which suppresses genetic mutations). Thus, it was shown that the constitutive over expression of the reverse transcriptase (telomerase subunit) with increased activity of key tumor suppressor listed above leads to a significant increase in median survival and slower aging of various parameters, in particular, skin and intestine.

Cellular aging can be reversed in telomerase positive cells such as the stem cells, and therefore, decline the number of stem cells is one of the causes of age-related disorders of the regenerative capacity of the body.

The following facts indicate that cellular aging –replicative and stress-induced, as well as the reduction of proliferating cells in general and stem, in particular, lead to disruption of regenerative capacity of tissues, and due to the age-dependent activation of apoptosis in a number of tissues result in de-generative disorders, which reduces the functionality of the organism.

Therefore, it is clear that the length of telo-meres is associated with the aging of the whole organism;

- Model organisms with telomerase de-fects are characterized by accelerated aging and reduced life expectancy
- Some of the symptoms of accelerated aging in humans are associated with premature telomere dysfunction
- Senescent cells are capable of destroying the extracellular matrix, as well as to in-duce local inflammation and tumor gene-sis
- Decreased or loss of proliferative capac-ity of stem cells during aging reduces the regenerative ability of any tissue of the body.

Astralgus & Telomerase

Telomeres are extremely important in aging process. At birth, there are about 8000 base pairs in length, but at the age of 65, they reduce up to 1500 pairs.

Each cell division shortens the length of the telomeres, which means we grow old genetically every single second. On the other hand, these telomeres are responsible in lengthening the lifespan. Therefore, it has always been an interesting topic how to stop or reverse the process of telomere shortening.

With the recognition of telomerase enzymes, many scientists were eager to find out how they can produce a supplement which can enhance the activity of telomerase.

Here comes the great discovery of the hidden secret of thousands of years. Astralgus, the most widely spoken natural plant, had its own magical component to solving the problem of aging, longevity, anti-cancer effect and prevention of many other diseases.

Stress, diet, and lifestyle can greatly affect the telomere length. Hence, when it comes to that extra help of battling the telomere shortening, Astralgus or Astralgus extracts have become the most popular supplement on earth. Astralgus has an ability to increase telomere length, protects telomere length and decrease the effects of aging, genetic mutations, and longevity.

TA-65 is a well-known telomerase activator. It contains a natural polymer called as hTERT, which activates telomerase. Thereby, it inhibits telomere shortening. More than 75% of people who used this TA-65 supplement stated that there was a significant improvement of their skin and immune functions. Also over 50% saw a great improvement in vision, libido, and quality of sleep.

TA-65 is an extract of Astralgus propinquus and even though it was a well-known herb in Chinese history, now Astralgus is known as a highly active telomerase activator.

Many debate that TA-65 contains cycloastrogenol, which is believed to be the active ingredients that is responsible for telomerase activation and this compound is extracted from Astralgus as well. Therefore, people who take cycloastrogenol supplements recommend adding Astralgus extract as well. They believe that synergetic activities of both supplements may increase the affectivity of telomerase activation.

Astralgus also contain astragalosides, which is also recognized as a potent stimulator of telomerase production.

Astralgus extract can be purchased as a powder, capsule or a liquid in health food stores. Many physicians agree on using Astralgus root extract as a health supplement to be taken by adults. But, it is always important to remember that pregnant and nursing women should consult their doctors before taking such a supplement.

Astralgus: The Plant

Astralgus is a plant genus which has about 3000 species of herbs and small shrubs. They belong to the family Fabaceae and the sub-family Faboidaea. Astralgus is the largest genus described.

These plants are native to temperate regions, especially in the northern hemisphere. They are also recognized as milkvetch by most of the people. In North America, some AStralgus species are called as locoweed and goat's thorn. Sometimes these Astralgus plants are difficult to differentiate from the vetches. But, normally vetches can be recognized as they are more vine-like.

Astralgus species are food for many larvae of some insect species called Lepidoptera.

'Tragacanth', the natural gum is made from several Astralgus species which grow in the Middle East. They are A. gummifer, A. adscendens, A. brachycalyx, A. tragacanthus and also A. adscendens. Astralgus membranaceus has a long history of being used in herbal medicine and traditional Chinese medicine and Persian medicine.

It is believed that Astralgus can highly improve the 'wei qi' or 'chi', which means 'life force' or 'energy flow'. The uses of this plant are so popular and have many records in Chinese history. But, it was not a subject of scientific study until 1980.

In the recent years this plant 'Astralgus' grabs the attention of many scientists and they believe that this is the great secret for the biggest revolution in modern medicine. Hence, there are many researches done in order to recognize the hidden health benefits and hidden miraculous chemical components.

Now many biotechnology firms are working on searching for a telomerase activator which can be derived from Astralgus. This came to a sudden interest after some studies recognized the chemical constituent cycloastrsgenol which is also known as TAT2 can help combat HIV (Human Immunodeficiency Virus) and also other chronic infections aging.

The researchers are being continuously done on this matter while many people started using Astralgus to treat several serious health conditions. The statistics and complementary medicine show that the results of using this plant have a higher rate of success.

While we know that Astralgus can be used as a medicinal plant; some species of Astralgus are used as an ornament or ornament making. They are A. alpines which has a bluish purple flower, A. hypoglottis with a purple flower and A. Lotoides. They are also grown in gardens as a beautiful gardening plant.

Atralgus membranecus

This plant can be found in Southeast East Asia, Dauria, Buryatia. The plants grow widely in these areas and are used in folk medicine in many countries: Tibet, Chinese, Mongolian, and Korean, as well as in Siberia.

The chemical composition of Astralgus:

Roots and rhizomes of Astralgus membranaceus contain triterpene saponins (astragaloside, O-astragalozoid, soyasaponiny, isoastragalasoides, soyasapogenol, cycloastragenol-6 glucopyranoside), triterpenoids, glucosides isoflavones, steroids, nitrogen, lignans, carbohydrates (sucrose, astragalany) pterokarpany, coumarins, vitamins C, D (tocopherol), A (Carotene) and E.

Also, the root of Astralgus membranecus contains macro–and micro elements such as iron, calcium, aluminum, cobalt, zinc, copper, vanadium, phosphorus, sodium and selenium up to 2.5 mg. The main feature is that this plant has a lot of selenium stored, and selenium is essential for the metabolism of living organisms as it is the trace mineral that promotes the mechanisms of blood cells production.

The therapeutic effects:

We can talk about selenium's effects on the body endlessly. Chinese scholars spoke about the benefits of selenium for the first time at the end of the 70s of the last century. They found that this substance is able to heal disease of the heart muscle in young women and children. Further studies have shown that Astralgus root is able to normalize the heart activities in people of all ages and also it helps in the strengthening of vascular walls. It also can extend the youth of the whole organism. Today selenium is also recommended for diseases of the liver and the entire digestive system.

In general, the lack of selenium is recommended to be fulfilled in order to have a healthy life. Lack of selenium in the body may lead to many diseases as selenium is a highly effective bio-corrector. Selenium does not only slow down the aging process but also reverse it, by increasing the activity of the stem cells.

Selenium helps our body in many other ways;

- Protect cells from free radicals
- Increased physical activity
- Prevent headaches and dizziness,
- Improves sleep, mood, and appetite.
- Participates in the synthesis of coenzyme Q-10,
- Improves skin, hair and nails.

- Normalizes activity of the thyroid hormones.

Selenium is the main component of the enzyme glutathione peroxidase (Glutathione), which protects the body from harmful substances formed during metabolic reactions. Selenium is an antagonist of mercury and arsenic and can protect the body from heavy metals such as cadmium, lead, thallium. It is also indicated for family planning and administered to both spouses. It is recommended to take selenium for women during pregnancy and lactation.

The herb Astralgus naturally accumulates organic selenium methionine about 5000 times more than any other herb. Natural syrups Astralgus have no side effects and contraindications and hence is recommended from the first year of life until the old age.

The natural form – selenomethionine is the most preferred for the body due to the high digestibility of 95-98%. While animal form of selenium is absorbed only by 30%, the inorganic form of selenium –10%.

The daily dose of 80-200 mcg of selenium is given for adults in the form of selenium-methionine or selenium-cysteine. In periods of high stress, as well as in various diseases –the daily rate shall be adjusted up to 800-1200 mcg. A deficiency of selenium can be manifested most often as diseases of the skin, hair, nails, immunodeficiency, inflammatory diseases of the joints, allergies, reducing protein synthesis and detoxification functions of the liver and as degenerative changes in the myocardium and muscles in general.

Astralgus has a healing effect when given as a comprehensive treatment medication for cardiomyopathy of different etiology, hepatitis, pancreatitis, diseases skin, ear, nose, and throat, etc.

Therapeutic agents of the roots of Astralgus membranaceus have a tonic effect; they stimulate blood cells synthesis, analgesic effect, and diuretic action. Externally Astralgus membranaceus is used as a wound healing substance and also this plant is recognized to have anticancer and antidiabetic effects. Moreover, infusions and decoctions of the roots of Astralgus are used as a choleretic, hemostatic, antipyretic, expectorant and diaphoretic. Scientifically it is proven that Astralgus has anti-hypertensive, diuretic, anti-oxidant, anti-tumor effect on human body. Polysaccharide fraction of this magical plant shows immune-stimulatory effects.

In Chinese medicine, Astralgus membranaceus is used in many products, as well as with ginseng (Panax ginseng) as a tonic for fatigue, general weakness, lack of appetite and spontaneous release from human sweat.

Effects of Astralgus are manifested by increasing the metabolism of the body, optimizing the functions of adrenal glands, reducing perspiration, acting as antibacterial, anticoagulant, antihypercholesterolemic, antihyper-glycemic, antihypertensive, antiseptic, antispasmodic, anti-tumor, antivirus (increases the production of interferon) and bactericidal. It also stimulates heart functions and has cardiotonic effects. Astralgus root can prevent colds, reduces protein fractions in urine, promotes digestion, strengthens the immune system and immunomodulatory and immunostimulant actions, improve endurance, increase and strengthen the metabolism, increase sperm motility, prevent flu, protects the liver and prevent diseases of the chest.

The chemical component really helps female and male sexual functions of the body, by increasing male libido and female menor-rhagias and metrorrhagias. In Chinese medicine, it is considered as a valuable and a special ability that Astralgus has to strengthen the function of sexual glands in both men and women. This property provides its rejuvenation in the hormonal level, which explains its intense use in eastern gerontology.

Astralgus preparations are indicated for:

- Diseases of the hematopoietic system; cardiovascular disease and hypertension;
- Diabetes and atherosclerosis;
- Diseases of the gastrointestinal tract and liver
- Malignancy (cancer) of all etiologies.
- Infectious diseases; it inhibits the development of bacterial and protozoa microflora (trichomonads, amoebas, etc.)
- The root powder is prescribed externally for boils, boils, abscesses, not only as

contributing to recent maturation but also as an antimicrobial.

- Abscess
- Adrenal disorders
- Aids
- Swelling of the legs,
- Loss of appetite,
- Joint pain, arthritis,
- Asthma, bronchitis, chronic lung weakness and runny nose,
- Cystitis, dysuria, nephritis, urethritis, urinary tract infections
- Weakness,
- Diabetes,
- Diarrhea, edema, and excessive sweating
- Fatigue and fever,
- Hepatitis,
- Immunodeficiency,
- Influenza and malaria
- Lymphangitis and lymphadenitis,
- Uterine bleeding,
- Dermatitis,

- Night sweats and numbness,

Even the ancient Aesculapius said that all diseases are interrelated, and one problem will inevitably lead others. Preventive effects of Astralgus allow complex healthier entire body, leading to beauty, health, strength and longevity.

Drug interactions of Astralgus:

Due to the diuretic action of this herb the following drug interactions are possible:

- May potentiate antidiabetic (hypoglycemic) drugs
- Increased risk of toxicity with anti-inflammatory analgesics;
- If hypokalemia occurs possible antagonism with antiarrhythmics and potentiation of muscle relaxants;
- May potentiate and –or interfere with antihypertensives;

- May potentiate lithium therapy;
- When taken with corticosteroids there is the risk of hypokalemia;
- May potentiate other diuretics and increase the risk of hypokalemia.
- Due to the cardioactive chemicals in this herb the following drug interactions:
  - Antagonism with antiarrhythmics
  - Antagonism of beta-adrenergic receptors
  - Potentiating of cardiac glycosides and increased risk of hypokalemia
  - When taken together with the depolarizing muscle relaxants, there is a risk of arrhythmia
  - Counteracts nitrates and calcium channel blockers; may increase the potential terafedina that can cause arrhythmia
- Due to the antihypertensive (hypotensive) action of this herb the following interactions are possible:

- When taken with anesthetics an increased hypotensive effect
- Potentiates the antihypertensive
- When taken with diuretics, it may end the difficulty with diuresis and hypertension
- Antagonism with sympathomimetics

Astralgus Dasyanthus

It is a perennial herbaceous plant of the legume family. It reaches a height of 40 cm. The Astralgus plant flowers in May and June. The flowers of this plant are yellow; they are collected in inflorescences, which are very dense. Fruits ripen in June and July.

Astralgus is common in the steppes of the European part of Russia. It grows mainly in open areas –for example, in open clearings in the forest. You can find it on the mounds and even old cemeteries. The cultivation of this plant in the garden is possible. Another name for this plant is "cat's peas." You cannot harvest too much of this plant, as it is prohibited.

The raw Astralgus roots are rarely used to take the medicinal material. The grass must be collected at a time when the plant is in bloom, it should be cut to a height of 10 cm from the ground level. When gathering should not damage the roots, as the plant dies from it. Dried material usually placed on an attic, under a canopy. The main thing should be that the room which stores Astralgus should be a well-ventilated room. Spreading the raw material into layer with a thickness of about 5 cm, it is periodically mixed. Then it is stored in a dry place. The shelf life of dried herbs is around 1 year.

The composition:

Grass plant contains flavonoids, tannins, steroids, organic acids. It is also noted that Astralgus contain a large amount of iron, essential oils, vitamins, calcium, phosphorus, manganese, and sodium. Also contains silicon, magnesium, and other trace elements. Astralgus can selectively accumulate selenium.

The health effects:

Astralgus Dasynathus has diuretic, hypotensive and sedative effect. It improves heart
function in patients; dilate the blood vessels
of the heart and blood vessels of the kidneys. The infusion has a positive effect on
the course of hypertension. Sometimes it is
used as an additional treatment of this disease.

Headaches can also be treated using this
plant, and it is used to reduce blood pressure
as well. In patients receiving Astralgus syrup,
the dizziness and heart pain disappear or decrease and also reduces tinnitus and neuro-
ses.

This herb is used for rinsing the mouth and
throat as it is effective in treating angina,
periodontal diseases, stomatitis and other
inflammatory processes. When applied topi-
cally, it has a wound-healing effect. It is

indicated in the treatment of chronic heart failure. It is recommended to patients suffering from vascular disorders of the kidneys.

The use of Astralgus leads to the expansion of the brain blood vessels and peripheral vessels, improves blood circulation and oxygen saturation of the internal organs.

Astralgus is very valued in folk medicine for its anti-tumor effect. It was confirmed by numerous herbalists in practice. It is also used to treat benign tumors (such as uterine fibroids and myomas) and malignancies (cancer of the ovary, breast, stomach, esophagus, throat, cervix, liver, and intestines). Astralgus eliminates excessive water retention with edema and prevents cerebral edema.

It is applied as a medication for edema, articular rheumatism, muscular dystrophy and poisoning. For many years, Astralgus is effectively used for the normalization of blood coagulation, normalization of capillary blood flow and to reduce the constriction of capillaries. Astralgus dasyanthus relieves shortness of breath and cyanosis and also increases urine output in patients.

Astralgus –is an effective hypotensive, wound healing, hemostatic, diuretic, vasodilator and cardiotonic agent.

Contraindications:

Astralgus should not be taken by the people who are allergic to this plant. Always make sure that you try these supplements under the supervision of a physician if you are suffering from any chronic heart disease. In any case, you need to very closely monitor the reaction of the organism. It is believed that high doses of Astralgus are dangerous.

Astralgus Recipes

Weakness and fatigue:

This condition occurs in the elderly and in children as a sign of the age of transition. This can also occur after prolonged illness and ischemia or angina, heart failure and inflammation of the kidneys.

In this state, you need to make a decoction of herbs astralgus 20 g of dry grass boiled with 200 grams of water, boil 10 minutes, drain. Drink 1 tablespoon from one to five times a day, depending on the severity of the condition.

Astralgus and brain hematoma:

As a supplement to the basic treatment, you can try out this recipe: 1 tbsp dry grass, pour a glass of boiled water and keep in a thermos or under the heat up to three hours. Drink 1 tablespoon up to four times a day, 15 minutes before meals in combination with honey. This will increase the anti-inflammatory effect and enrich the body microelements.

Astralgus with pneumonia, inflammation of the respiratory tract:

In these diseases, a decoction of Astralgus drink would be perfect: Boil 1 tablespoon of dry Astralgus grass with a glass of boiling water for 10 minutes. Strain and drink 1 tbsp five times per day. The same recipe will help with atherosclerosis, heart disease –and myocarditis, as well as for the prevention of high blood pressure.

Astralgus and liver disease:

100 g of boiling water cook 20g of dry grass for 10 minutes, then cool and drink 1 tablespoon five times per day.

Swelling and edema of the brain, cancerous brain tumor:

These serious diseases are best treated with the infusions of Astralgus: In a thermos boil a glass of water with 1 tablespoon of dry grass for 2 hours. Drink 1 tablespoon 15 minutes before a meal, 4 times a day.

Gastric ulcer and 12 duodenal ulcer:

Add 200g of honey and 20g of dry Astralgus grass in water and boil for 10 minutes. Let it cool down. Then drink this infusion. Drink 3-5 tablespoons with a glass of warm milk. This infusion can be refrigerated for further use. It is also possible to dissolve it in warm water

(5 spoonfuls of 0.5 liters and drink in small sips throughout the day). Infusion of honey can be stored in the refrigerator.

There is a second recipe to help get rid of these diseases: Add 20g of Astralgus grass in 0.5 liters of milk and simmer in a slightly heated stove in a ceramic or glass container for half an hour. Then add two cups of honey (400 g) and heat for another 10 minutes, stirring occasionally with a wooden spoon. Remove from the stove and then let it cool. Pour into a glass dish. This can be stored in the refrigerator.

Astralgus in breast cancers and skin:

Here you can apply externayl: Add 200g of honey and 20g of dry Astralgus grass in water and boil for 10 minutes. Let it cool down. Apply this on affected areas.

Brain tumor, swelling, edema, and high blood pressure:

There used alcohol tincture of Astralgus: 30 g of Astralgus grass add in 0.5 liters of alcohol or vodka for two weeks. Thus, it is necessary to shake the tincture daily, preferably several times a day, to use all liquid passed into the grass. After 2 weeks drain and refrigerate. This should be administered as 25 drops with 2 tbsp water, taken several times a day. If the disease is severe, the dose can be increased up to 50 drops.

TA-65

Telomerase Activator TA-65 is an anti-aging product in the form of a dietary supplement, which, according to the manufacturer, is able to significantly rejuvenate all the major systems of the body, alleviate the condition of patients suffering from diabetes, Alzheimer's disease and serious cardiovascular pathologies.

The developer is a well-known American company Geron Corporation, which is engaged in research in the field of biotechnology since 1990 (including its projects –preparations for the treatment of cancer affecting telomerase, and products based on stem cells to treat spinal cord injuries). In 2002, Geron transferred the rights to distribute the Activator TA-65 of Telomerase Activation Science (TA Science), Inc.

The active ingredient is cycloastragenol BUD –an extract of the root of membranous milk vetch (Astralgus membranaceus). In addition to the data Geron and TA Science, the ability to activate telomerase cycloastragenol was confirmed in 2009 by a team of biologists and biochemists in California under the direction of Hector Valenzuela. However, the only study that proves the effectiveness of the use of the drug for this purpose in the form of a food additive was carried out by the same TA Science in 2005 – since then for nearly a decade of new scientific evidence of this fact is not presented.

TA-65 –means of natural origin, the effectiveness of which has been confirmed by independent laboratory tests and the results of clinical observations. TA-65 activates the telomerase enzyme and starts the recovery process of critically short telomeres in a cell, slowing aging.

The effects of TA-65 supplements are:

- Reducing the risk of age-related diseases and cancer
- The rejuvenation of the immune system
- Maintaining cognitive functions (memory, attention, and mental abilities)
- Increased skin elasticity
- Improving the condition of hair and nails
- Improving the quality of
- Preservation and maintenance of sexual energy
- Increased bone density